Wildlife Watchers

Birds

Terry Jennings

QED

Copyright © QED Publishing 2009

First published in the UK in 2009 by
QED Publishing
A Quarto Group Company
226 City Road
London EC1V 2TT

www.qed-publishing.co.uk

ISBN 978 1 84835 233 9

Author Terry Jennings
Consultant Steve Parker
Project Editor Eve Marleau
Designer and Picture Researcher
    Liz Wiffen

Publisher Steve Evans
Creative Director Zeta Davies
Managing Editor Amanda Askew

Printed and bound in China

Picture credits
Key: t=top, b=bottom, r=right, l=left, c=centre

Alamy 11b Andrew Darrington, 17r Curt and
Cary Given

IStock 26b johnandersonphoto

NHPA 4r Martin Harvey, 9c Manfred
Danegger, 13t Alan Williams, 13b Laurie
Campbell, 14c Bill Coster, 15t Bill Coster,
18c Jaanus Jarva, 19t Bill Coster, 19b Richard
Kuzminski, 21l Rupert Buchele, 22c Lee Dalton,
27r David Tipling, 28t Martin Harvey,
29l Martin Wendler, 29r Martin Harvey,
31b Rupert Buchele

Shutterstock 2r iofoto, 3r iNNOCENt,
4c Steve Byland, 5c Christopher Ewing,
5b Milos Luzanin, 6r Morgan Lane
Photography, 7l David Dohnal, 8r iNNOCENt,
9t Tony Campbell, 10c Andrew Williams,
10b W. Woyke, 11tdr. Le Thanh Hung,
11r Santiago Cornejo, 11b Christian Musat,
12c David Dohnal, 15b Hydromet, 16r Ivonne
Wierink, 17l Gertjan Hooijer, 20c Uwe Ohse,
21r Verena Lüdemann, 21b Peter Elvidge,
23t Kenneth William Caleno, 23b Joel
Calheiros, 24r iofoto, 25t Tom Curtis,
25b David Dohnal, 27c Jason Vandehey,
27b Timothey Kosachev

StockXchange 20–21 ElvisSantana,
28–29 Kriss Szkurlatowski

The words in **bold**
are explained in the
glossary on page 30.

Contents

What is a bird?

Birds are the only animals that have feathers. A bony **skeleton** supports their body. They lay eggs with a hard shell. Most birds build **nests** to keep their eggs and young safe and sheltered. Birds can live all over the world.

Scrape

Hole nest

➡ Ostriches are the largest birds in the world.

Nests

Nests come in many shapes and sizes. Most nests are cup shaped and are built in trees and bushes, but others are dome shaped. Some birds make nests on the ground or on beaches. This kind of nest is called a scrape. Some nests are built on the sides of buildings, or in holes in trees and are called hole nests. Nests are made of many materials, including sticks and mud.

Dome-shaped nest

Cup-shaped nest

Did you know?

There are more than 9000 different species, or kinds, of bird. The largest bird is the ostrich. It can grow up to 2.5 metres in height, and its eggs can weigh up to 1.8 kilograms.

Legs, wings and beaks

All birds have wings, but some birds, such as penguins, cannot fly. A bird's legs are covered in **scales**. Scales are flat, hard pieces of skin that overlap each other. Birds have hard beaks, but their mouths are soft inside, like a human's. Birds use their beaks to pick up things and clean themselves.

Flight feathers

↑ Although penguins cannot fly, they use their wings as paddles when they swim underwater.

Beak

➡ Doves are strong fliers. Their flight feathers push and steer them through the air.

Body feathers

Tail feathers

Scaly legs and clawed feet

Body feather

Down feather

Flight feather

Feathers

Feathers are made of the same material as a human hair and fingernails. There are three main types of feather. Down feathers grow close to the skin and help to keep the bird warm. Body feathers cover the bird like a waterproof jacket and give it a **streamlined** shape. Flight feathers on the wings and tail help the bird to fly.

Be a bird watcher

You can be a bird watcher whether you live in a town or city or in the countryside. You can even study the birds you see on your way to and from school.

Equipment

These are the main items you will need for birdwatching:

- Notebook
- Pen or pencil
- Binoculars to make the bird seem much nearer

⬇ **U**se binoculars to see birds more clearly when you go out birdwatching.

Binoculars

Did you know?

The vervain hummingbird of Jamaica lays the world's smallest egg. It is about the size of a small pea.

Identifying birds

You can identify different species of bird by looking at their shapes, colours and markings. A garden or park is a good place to start birdwatching. Once you have identified a bird, you could make a table in your notebook to record your findings.

↑ When you see a bird, draw a simple sketch in your notebook. You can add details about the bird's colours and markings.

Close-up with binoculars

Date	Type of bird	Time of day	Place	Kind of weather	What was the bird doing?	Was the bird alone?
2nd March	Magpie	10 a.m.	The park	Sunny	Sitting in the trees	In a pair
28th April	Coot	3.30 p.m.	The river	Breezy	Swimming	Yes
18th July	Barn owl	7.30 p.m.	The woods	Warm	Flying	Yes

WARNING!

Always tell an adult when and where you are going birdwatching, and never leave the adult you are with without permission.

Carry a spare pen or pencil, just in case you need it

HB

City birds

Some birds live in busy towns and cities. They often feed on the scraps of food that people put out for them. You can see these birds in the countryside as well.

Am I quite fat with a short tail? Am I mostly blue—grey, or even white in colour?

Small head

Rounded body

Spotting city birds

W **Feral** pigeons often live in large numbers. They are seen on city buildings and in parks and gardens, often feeding on scraps of food.

W Starlings can be seen in many places, walking on the ground as they look for insects and grubs. In summer, starlings often gather together in **flocks** of thousands.

W Magpies are often seen in pairs, crowing, or calling, in the trees. Some people do not like them because they kill and eat baby birds. However, most of their food comes from animals that have been killed on the road.

Feral pigeon

Length: 31–35 cm
Habitat: Cities, towns, ruined buildings, farms
Food: Human food scraps, seeds, garden plants
Nest: On ledges on buildings
Eggs: 2, but breed all year round

Am I quite large with a short beak? Am I black and white? Do I have a long tail?

Long, green–black tail

White patch on wing

Blue–black wing

Yellow beak

Am I quite small? Do I have a thin beak and green or purple feathers with spots on?

Spotted breast

Magpie

Length: 42–50 cm
Habitat: Parks, gardens, grassland with trees, farmland, woodland, by the sea
Food: Insects, slugs, worms, small birds, grains, fruit, dead animals, or **carrion**
Nest: Large domed nest of sticks in a tree or thorn bush
Eggs: 5–7

Starling

Length: 20.5–23.5 cm
Habitat: Towns, cities, farmland, cliffs, woodland
Food: Insects, seeds, berries, fruit, grains, human food scraps
Nest: In holes in trees and buildings and under climbing plants
Eggs: 4–7

Watch it!

Which foods do birds like best? Choose some different foods, such as seeds and bread, and put each kind of food in a dish. Put the dishes outside. Which food is eaten first?

Small birds with short beaks

Many small birds have strong, short beaks. They use their beaks to crack open seeds. These birds will eat other foods, too, particularly in winter when they are hungry.

> Am I quite small with a brown beak and a grey head?

Grey head

Pale eyebrow

Black bib

MALE

> Am I small with a brown beak and a dull, grey underside?

Dull, grey underside

Spotting small birds with short beaks

🐾 House sparrows live in flocks. The male has a small, black spot underneath its beak that looks like a baby's bib.

🐾 In winter, tree sparrows sometimes join flocks of house sparrows and other small birds.

🐾 The male chaffinch has a grey-blue top to his head and a pink chest. The female is duller in colour.

House sparrow

Length: 14–15.5 cm
Habitat: Houses, farms, parks and gardens
Food: Human food scraps, seeds, insects
Nest: In holes, or in ivy or other thick plant growth
Eggs: 3–6

FEMALE

Am I small with a brown top to my head? Do I have a black patch on my cheek?

Brown head

Black cheek patch

Tree sparrow
Length: 13.5–14.5 cm
Habitat: Old trees, ruined buildings, cliffs
Food: Seeds and insects
Nest: Mostly in holes in trees
Eggs: 4–6

Am I small with a white patch on my shoulder and a white stripe on my wings?

Grey-blue head

White stripe

Pink chest

White shoulder

MALE

Am I small with a white stripe on my wings?

Chaffinch
Length: 14.5–16 cm
Habitat: Parks, gardens, woods, hedges, farmland in winter
Food: Seeds, fruit, insects
Nest: Small cup-shaped nest in bushes and trees
Eggs: 4–5

White stripe

WARNING!

If birds live near your home, don't go near their nest. The parent birds may leave the nest because they are scared, and never come back to their babies.

FEMALE

11

Small birds with thin beaks

Birds with short, thin beaks mainly use them for picking up insects and insect grubs. If they are really hungry, they will eat other foods, too, such as seeds and berries.

Am I very small and brown? Do I have a short, turned-up tail?

Turned-up tail

Brown colouring

Spotting small birds with thin beaks

Wrens are small, active birds that move quickly on the ground like mice. Their song is very loud for such a tiny bird.

Song thrushes crack open snail shells by beating them on a stone. They then use their beak to pull out the animal inside the shell before eating it.

Long-tailed tits build an oval nest made of moss and lichens and lined with feathers. The nest has a hole in the side.

Wren

Length: 9–10 cm
Habitat: Gardens, parks, woods, farmland, bushes, hedges, cliffs
Food: Insects, seeds
Nest: Domed nest in hedges or ivy, and in crevices, or cracks
Eggs: 5–8

Pink shoulders

Am I very small and light coloured underneath? Do I have a long, narrow tail?

Long, narrow tail

Long-tailed tit

Length: 13.5–14.5 cm
Habitat: Edges of woods and forests, thick hedges, parks
Food: Insects and seeds
Nest: Oval ball in a thorny bush or high up a tree
Eggs: 7–12

 Do I have a brown back and a light-coloured underside covered in dark spots?

Brown back

Spotted underside

Song thrush

Length: 22–24 cm
Habitat: Gardens, parks, thick hedges, woods, bushes
Food: Snails, slugs, worms, insects, berries
Nest: Cup-shaped nest in hedges, trees, ivy and sheds
Eggs: 4–6

Watch it!

Make a bird bath using a shallow bowl. Sink the bowl into the ground before you fill it with clean water. Record which birds come to bathe or drink.

13

Birds with forked tails

Some birds have forked tails. Their tails separate into two points at the end, instead of being one whole section. As winter approaches, birds with forked tails fly to warmer countries. This is called **migration**.

Am I a blue–black colour with a white underside? Do I have a short, forked tail?

White underside

Short, forked tail

Spotting birds with forked tails

- Swifts have weak legs, so they cannot walk on the ground. They take off from high places to jump straight into the air.

- House martins build nests under the **eaves** of buildings such as houses and barns, under bridges and on cliffs.

- Swallows build nests in barns, on ledges and in rafters. They sometimes hunt over water.

House martin
Length: 12–13 cm
Habitat: Towns, villages, bridges, cliffs
Food: Flying insects
Nest: Nest made of mud, under house eaves and bridges, or on cliffs
Eggs: 4–5

Birds of prey ?

Am I very large, with long wings and a rounded tail? Do I fly high in the sky and glide a long way?

Pale head and neck

Birds of prey hunt during the day. They have a hooked beak for tearing off flesh. They also have long, sharp claws, called **talons**, that they use to catch and hold their **prey**.

Dark-brown back

Spotting birds of prey

- Golden eagles live in lonely places where there are few people around, such as on mountains or cliffs by the sea.

- Kestrels hunt over farmland, meadows, parks, towns, moors and marshes.

- When hunting their prey, peregrine falcons are the fastest-flying birds in the world.

Large talon

Golden eagle

Length: 76–90 cm
Habitat: Mountains, moorland, hills, cliffs, pine forests
Food: Small mammals, birds, carrion
Nest: Big pile of sticks and twigs on cliffs or in trees
Eggs: 2

Birds of the night

Most birds are active during the day and, like us, they sleep at night. However, there are a few birds that are **nocturnal**, or awake at night.

Am I a large brown and black owl with 'ears' on the top of my head?

Ear tuft

Orange eye

Hooked beak

Talon

Spotting owls

Ψ Many owls are nocturnal. All owls have extremely good eyesight and hearing. Unlike most birds, owls have eyes that face forwards.

Ψ Owls can turn their heads all the way around so that they can see behind them.

Ψ Many owls have feathers that match their surroundings, so they are hard to see when they are resting. This is called **camouflage**.

Long-eared owl

Length: 34–37 cm
Habitat: Woods, forests, moors, marshes
Food: Small mammals, birds, insects
Nest: In old birds' or squirrels' nests, such as those of magpies, or on the ground
Eggs: 3–6

Water birds

Am I quite large and mainly black in colour? Do I have a white patch at the front of my head?

Many different kinds of bird live near water. Some of them can walk across water plants. Others dive under the water to catch food. Some have long legs so they can walk through water, while a few have long necks that help them reach water plants and animals underwater.

White patch

Lobed foot

Spotting water birds

🌿 Herons stand in shallow water looking for food. They nest high up in trees in groups called heronries.

🌿 Coots live on lakes and rivers in the town and countryside. They have strange lobed, or rounded, feet that help them to swim and dive.

🌿 Dippers feed by diving or walking underwater on the bottoms of streams and shallow rivers. They look for water insects and other small animals.

Coot

Length: 36–40 cm
Habitat: Lakes, rivers and reservoirs
Food: Mainly water plants, but also insects, water snails, tadpoles and fish eggs
Nest: Built in reeds or rushes and resting on the water
Eggs: 4–8

Am I small and dark brown with a white throat and chest? Am I in or near a fast-flowing river or stream?

Sharp beak

Am I large and mainly grey in colour? Do I have a very long neck, long legs and a large, sharp beak?

White throat

Short tail

Long neck

Dipper
Length: 17–18.5 cm
Habitat: Fast-flowing streams and rivers
Food: Water insects and other small animals
Nest: Domed nest on ledges or near water
Eggs: 4–6

Grey heron
Length: 90–100 cm
Habitat: Rivers, lakes, marshes, estuaries
Food: Fish, frogs, voles, insects
Nest: Nests in a herony in tall trees, sometimes far from water
Eggs: 3–5

Baby coot

Did you know?
Baby coots are black and fluffy with bright-red heads. They can swim as soon as they hatch.

Long legs

21

Ducks, geese and swans ?

Am I very large with a black head, long, black neck and a white patch under my chin?

Ducks, geese and swans are large birds that live on or near water. They mainly live near lakes, ponds and rivers, but some also live near salt-water areas such as the sea.

White patch

Black head

Brown back

Spotting ducks, geese and swans

- Mallards are the most common ducks in the city and countryside.
- Canada geese are often seen in large, noisy flocks. The goslings, or babies, are green-yellow or brown in colour.
- Swans have huge wings, and when they fly they make a swishing sound.

Canada goose

Length: 90–110 cm
Habitat: Lakes, rivers, marshes and farmland
Food: Grass, water plants
Nest: Made of weeds
Eggs: 5–7

Do I have a shiny green head and a black tail?

Curly tail feather

Green head

Am I brown with a yellow beak?

FEMALE

MALE

Yellow beak

Mallard

Length: 55-62 cm
Habitat: Any fresh or salt water
Food: Seeds, plants, small animals
Nest: In sheltered spots on the ground or in holes in trees
Eggs: 9-12

Am I very large and white in colour? Do I have a long neck and an orange beak?

Long, curved neck

Orange beak

Mute swan

Length: 145-160 cm
Habitat: Any fresh or salt water, including lakes, rivers, marshes, bays, estuaries
Food: Water plants and grass
Nest: On banks, in marshes or among reeds
Eggs: 2-9

Did you know?
Mute swans can live for more than 20 years.

Seabirds

The sea can be a difficult place for a bird to live. Storms, winds and huge waves are very dangerous. Some seabirds spend their lives out at sea, only coming on land to lay their eggs.

Am I quite large and mostly white, with a dark—brown head and a dark—red beak and legs?

?

Dark—brown head

Dark—red legs

Red beak

Spotting seabirds

🐾 Black-headed gulls are one of many kinds of gull. In winter they come inland and their heads become mainly white.

🐾 The oystercatcher is common on the seashore where it can feed on shellfish, small crabs and other small creatures that live in the mud or sand.

🐾 Puffins nest in colonies. They either dig their burrows themselves, or take over rabbits' burrows.

Black—headed gull

Length: 35–38 cm
Habitat: By the sea, rivers and lakes, on farmland and in city parks
Food: Small sea and land animals, seeds, scraps
Nest: Mostly in long grass by water
Eggs: 2–3

Am I mostly black and white with orange feet? Do I have a huge red, yellow and blue beak?

Large, triangular beak

White face

Am I quite large and mostly black and white? Do I have pink legs and a long, orange beak?

Puffin
Length: 29–31 cm
Habitat: By the sea and on cliffs
Food: Fish and small sea animals
Nest: In a colony of burrows on cliffs by the sea
Eggs: 1

Orange leg and foot

Long, orange beak

Pink leg

Oystercatcher
Length: 41–45 cm
Habitat: Mainly on sandy and muddy shores
Food: Small animals living in sand, mud and soil
Nest: A scrape on sand or in grass
Eggs: 2–4

Watch it!

If you see a bird's footprints by the seashore, take a photograph of them. You can look in a field guide to see which bird they belong to.

Woodland birds

Many birds live in woods and forests. They adapted, or changed, a long time ago to live in these places. Birds that climb trees have toes that allow them to cling to tree trunks. Birds that live on the ground are camouflaged among the grass and leaves.

Spotting woodland birds

- Woodcocks use their beaks to search for food. They stick them into soft ground to search for insects and other bugs.

- Although crossbills will eat other seeds, they mainly eat the seeds inside cones.

- Treecreepers have large claws and a long tail. Their slightly curved beak helps them to find insects and grubs in tree bark.

Am I a red-brown colour all over with broad, dark stripes on the back of my head?

Woodcock
Length: 32-36 cm
Habitat: Woodland and forest clearings with damp areas
Food: Worms, insects, spiders, centipedes
Nest: A leaf-lined scrape on the ground, under brambles or ferns
Eggs: 4

Dark stripes

Long beak

Red-brown feathers

Short leg

Fill a string bag (like those supermarkets sell onions in) with dried grass. Hang the bag from a tree. Push sticks into the bag to act as perches. Which birds come to your bag for nesting materials?

Am I small and brown with a long tail? Do I creep up tree trunks?

Long, curved beak

Treecreeper
Length: 12–13 cm
Habitat: woods, parks and gardens
Food: Insects, small bugs
Nest: Behind tree bark or ivy, or in cracks in tree trunks
Eggs: 5–6

Spotted feathers

Large claw

Am I high up in trees that have cones? Am I mostly red? Do I have a beak where the two tips overlap?

Crossed beak

Am I small and green in colour? Do the tips of my beak overlap?

Crossbill
Length: 16–17 cm
Habitat: Conifers, especially in woods and forests, but also in parks and gardens
Food: Conifer seeds, but also berries, thistle seeds and insects
Nest: Cup-shaped nest high in conifers
Eggs: 3–4

MALE

FEMALE

Green feathers

Birds in danger

Many kinds of bird are in danger of dying out altogether. This is called **extinction**. Most of these birds are facing extinction because of things that human beings do.

Habitat loss

All over the world, people are destroying **habitats**, or places where birds live. Woods and forests are being cleared to provide land for farms, roads, houses and factories. When these places are destroyed, the birds that lived there have nowhere to feed or breed.

➡ When forests are cut down, the birds that live and breed there have to find somewhere else to go.

➡ In the future, some birds will not be able to live in the places where they do now. This is because of the effects of **pollution** on the Earth.

28

Hunting and collecting

In some parts of the world, many birds are killed for their meat, for their beautiful feathers, or just for fun. Some people collect wild birds to keep as pets, while other people make collections of birds' eggs.

←These parrots have been captured for their feathers or to be kept as pets.

Pollution

Many birds have been killed by chemicals used on farms to kill pests or to make crops grow better. At sea, oil spilled from ships kills thousands of birds every year. Litter can be harmful to wildlife. Plastic rings from packs of drinks can sometimes choke birds.

➡This oil-soaked penguin has been rescued. If its feathers can be cleaned, it may survive.

Glossary

Camouflage A way of hiding in which the animal looks like its surroundings.

Carrion The flesh of dead animals.

Eaves The space between the walls and the roof of a building.

Extinction Not in existence any more. A species is extinct when no members of it are left alive.

Feral A pet or farm bird that now lives in the wild.

Flock A group of birds.

Habitat Where a plant or animal lives.

Migration The long journey animals make, at certain times, in search of food, a warmer climate or somewhere to breed.

Nest The place where a bird lays its eggs.

Nocturnal Mainly active at night.

Pollution Harmful substances that damage the environment.

Prey An animal hunted and eaten by another animal.

Scales Small, flat pieces of skin that overlap each other.

Skeleton The framework of bones inside an animal's body.

Species Any one kind of animal or plant.

Streamlined Shaped to move smoothly and quickly through air or water.

Talon The claw of a bird of prey.

Index

Notes for parents and teachers

When you help a child to identify birds, bear in mind that only a tiny proportion of the total number of species can be shown in this book. A reference book for the birds of your local area, illustrated by clear pictures, may be helpful.

A visit to a zoo, wildlife park, safari park or some other collection of living birds will help children to appreciate the great diversity of bird life in the world today.

A simple bird table or bird feeder is quite easy for a child to make, with adult help, or relatively inexpensive to buy. Such bird tables and bird feeders provide an excellent way for children to study common birds closely.

A number of safety precautions are necessary when children study birds. They should not handle living or dead wild birds, as they often are host to disease organisms or parasites. Children should always wash their hands thoroughly after handling food remains, bird feeders, bird baths or any other items or materials that wild birds have come into contact with.

* Website information is correct at time of going to press. However, the publishers cannot accept liability for any information or links found on third-party websites.

Even simple, inexpensive binoculars will help to make birds appear nearer. Children will need help at first in focusing the binoculars and in learning to look through them.

Some useful websites for more information:
www.bbc.co.uk/nature/animals/birds
www.enchantedlearning.com/subjects/birds/
www.kidwings.com/index.htm
www.rspb.org.uk
www.birdwatchin.com/birding_for_kids
http://kids.yahoo.com/animals/birds
www.nwf.org/wildlife